YOU HAVE NO RIGHT TO KILL

KILL

HUMANISM DIVERTED

MANI MOHAMED

INDIA • SINGAPORE • MALAYSIA

Notion Press

Old No. 38, New No. 6
McNichols Road, Chetpet
Chennai - 600 031

First Published by Notion Press 2019
Copyright © Mani Mohamed 2019
All Rights Reserved.

ISBN 978-1-64760-687-9

What is humanism???

"its loving and living with even a piece of life on this earth"

"Oru peeda urumbinum varutharudhu"

By Sree Narayana Guru

CONTENTS

HUMANISM RE-INTRODUCED TO REPRESENT THE EARTH

And **to humanism,** we proceed to fulfill the purpose of this universal saga of life's evolution from amoeba to the most intelligent and exclusive living organism in this universe. The **excursion of atoms** and molecules to unite and subjugate the needs and purposes of this expanding universe without proportionate to the organisms thus produced by the basic carbon, hydrogen, oxygen etc., marching into heavy metals and organic to a living organism and interactive living products with super mental and physical powers.

Thus we are the elite elusive, exclusive and elaborated species in this world or universe as a whole to express each and every tiny part and particle and participants of this universe.

Hence we are the prime product and without our existence the universe is void.

The imminent source of our existence is the immortal sense of our inner mind and inner body in a proportion of the then precipitated from the cosmological background by-product or the whey of the churning out of cosmological mass with a totalized functional product with basic water content.

So we humans are more important to the universe and our well being is the matter of every product that exists in this universe even if its God too.

So lets be good, so lets be humans, so lets play humanism, so lets game with humanity, so lets survive for humanity, so lets work out humanism, so lets drum for human co-existence, so lets grow for humanitarian socialism, so lets drive for ecological humanity. so lets brain drain for humanitarian causes in every single unit of the cultural, sociological, intelligent living hood, that the universe continues expanding to existence.

Hence this word of call. Hence this verse to recall. Hence this march to redraw

Hence this start emerges a new human race. lets give the start a quick start and call for

...You Have No Right To Kill!!!!

Human individuality is a matter of prevalence. As individual human is the contributor to the community of human race directly or indirectly to civilize and socialize the co-existence unlike the animal kingdom.

So lets make a change.. Not like the one which the scriptures have given us, not by the law of the land and not by the virtue of living style in an area. But by love and affection which shower brotherhood in the social existence.

Thus the leading light is love for the fellow being and the affection that one can shower on the fellow beings and the co-existing animals too. So living together in this universe is the prime aim of human race. HENCE THIS START....

THE LAWS

HUMANITY that was professed throughout the centuries through the thoughtful human individual or cult or human valued interpreter or human in prophetic attire. HHumanism was the talk since ever man had been thought out be civilized. Hence the humanitarian values were taught to the society to live together and endorse a living together society to be then established.

More and more people came with knowledge and guided the society and guidance became obedience to the learned men which lead them to be considered holy ones, prophets, Godly men and there came in the devoted people to these men or their advises and guidance to the straight path were endorsed. This carried out through centuries and into the strong fold of men in different value based living style and practice that came down. This let to group of people practicing under a particular individual being respected and with devotion which rendered and let the world to live in peace.

Then came in religious groups to replace these groups of men with Gods intervention at intervals in certain area of the world. Then came written manuscripts to keep going this process. Then followed suit by all religious links with or without known or unknown beginning of this religious walks through centuries. Off course there was a silent and salient thoughtful intelligent men living without these eternal intervention and belief, with no creator to this universe and humans called to be atheist.

Thus we find the differed practice, promotions and promises. Thus we find the solace in and out of the religious sectors too. Thus we find the rule and regulatory amendments with small variations to correct the last mistakes, Thus we find the stubborn natures in the practice and prayers that we now see a clash between the sector of religious in and out of the ring.

But even with all these are we are happy together and living peaceful. Now then we have started thinking out of context and formulated out of syllabus certain norms and clauses to make a law that can be a common practice and procedures to keep life going. Thus we see laws of monarchy, empires, statehood, country and larger continental law finally a internal linking law to abide by.

Thus we are large community with different opinions and laws ; but we live together with corrections of our mistakes. Sometimes by keeping with promise of peaceful life or by aggressive taunts to abide international laws to control the rogues.

Well with all these our nature and style of functioning of the rule and law has not changed since inception of human footsteps on this earth and we call ourselves the elite in the era of information super highway of knowledge enroot.

As eating cattle meat or pork is disliked by some community belief and on the other side it is just a food additive to the living being. And snakes are sacred and revered also rituals are attributed to its supremacy over other animals and on the other side it is eaten and even sold market as meat to quench human taste buds.

All these show that we are not in a situation to or able to cope-up with living habits too. There must be a common platform to rethink on eating habits too. Or a freewill to accept the both sides. Now it makes to itself dictate the very food habits of a common man. This is harmful to the society that it reflects in the physical and mental ability of human existence and stronghold in the human psychological deflections. Now come together to a common platform with common sense. So that we can change in the social set-up. Its time to groom a new society in the whole world.

THE LOSS

Everyone has the right to questioning any one individual or government or monarchy or any dictator too by verbal dialogue and they are answerable to. Not under the law of the land but on humanitarian ground. No more suppressions of questioning/speech or criticism or ideals generated in mind of common men's world.

So change yourself by now to gain life to the ethical system of human race which was defined by rulers and policies and political process even as through though monopolizing. Thus when every killings is consented by law ; every government is also answerable if its even punishable. No more dungeons /construction of concentration camps/no jails/no lock-ups for humans with crimes or mistakes. They have a stokehold in the society and the society has responsibility to dispel courtesy and kindness to the victims too. Solutions are to be found within limited span. We are not stone age people nor we are ice age animals and not even the final or last age people.

It is a combined effort and energy with quantum wisdom of all human race. So be not boasting on achievements. Its our duty towards human race and its not any obligation or not any service yet.

Hence the lost world has to be revived and restored WITH A NEW WORLD AND HUMANISM WITH COMPASSION at every single step ahead the coming centuries, So lets change ....so..

YOU HAVE NO RIGHT TO KILL!!!???

Dayaye Dharmadha Moolavaiah!! Said: Basavanna, the12th century Reformer.

Meaning = Compassion Is the Root of Religion.

CAPITAL LIFE ENFORCEMENT

There shall be a halt for capital punishment ; sometimes a full stop.!!!!!

A new method or approach worth of it or match the societal ill effective illegal practice being maintained throughout centuries and man could never think of an alternative, its quiet amazing. Well what if we Indians could rethink and make a change. Death!! which takes life has its potential grievance and partial connivance. Life is the most and foremost status that could be the source and enthusiasm that keeps the earthlings and earth alive and all the abundant resources to be reused.

Hence keeping alive one's life and others life to motivate and promote the events on earth is the ultimate goal of human race. The extinction of life of not only animals are at stake. The human race by the ethnic grace of human too are at stake. By restoring a life or bringing no sickness is our sole duty to run the show - that's the human race"

Life! none other less than is worth on this earth to sense the eagerness, or the expectation of a soul or body being put to cut -off or minced off or hanged -up or at intensive care by means of legal systems, by justification, by ethnic cleansing or by mowing or massacre or lynching or by even health hazards. This is the moment we are at and yet to recover and regain life's momentum. So to cut or a hit at life is a bad thing in human culture that's civilized or uncivilized.

Just let us make a change in our land as all changes were brought though us. We the moral society, religious and pious with social set–up, the Vedic chanting tongues, the dependents of spiritual life and the first to announce AHIMSA PARAMODHARMA can only do the this act. The only and most diversified cultural people of unity with divine water logs flowing ahead and joining the seas and oceans. Thus we start again with newest and neatest weapon for punishment. No eye for an eye. No shoot outs. No hanging by law and legal systems, or by governance or by rebellion or militancy.

WE INDIANS HAVE THE RIGHT TO START THAT …

DEATH SENTENCE

Death sentence in the broadest sense is defect in the nature of human social sentimental living habits. It has not deflected any kind of cruelty or any kind of harmful terrorizing behavior. It has been only a tool to divert the mentality of human in the time limit through frightening, cautioning to a certain limit. It has not been a tool to eradicate evil in the society. Hence we have to rethink of punishment and sentencing with capital punishment as by the rulers, the governance and militant outfits or terrorist.

Hanging is not the solution, killing is not only the process that can deter crime. The situation, surroundings, the political living scenario, the religious clutters, the nocturnal habitat, such as these things along with you and me too, is responsible for the crime. So these are crime generators.

According to Behaviorist B. F. Skinner, the psychologist who first described operant conditioning, identified two different kinds of aversive stimuli that can be used as punishment. While punishment can be effective in some cases, you can probably think of a few examples of when a punishment *does not* reduce a behavior. Prison is one example. After being sent to jail for a crime, people often continue committing crimes once they are released from prison.

So lets make a change to our social set-up with the elite and elaborate think tanks around us struggling to compromise with human life to sustain all injuries, ailing, sickness, diseases, major damages even through science and technology. In this era of wisdom and knowledge Bank(g)s and information highways, we are to make a change to the dark ages which has passed unto this generation. When mobiles goes 5 G and we remain in the minus-G as old as our ancestral stone age people. Rethinking in religious line too is essential. What the fundamental basic thought of religions or religious and spiritual life has given and prophesied has not been practiced till date. All blunders were equalized to religious practice and rituals beings the abstract of religious and caste systems, to divulge the entire thoughtful mental suppressions by the communities to be supreme to show supremacy over others.

Hanging is not the solution, killing is not the only process that can deter crime. Th situations and surroundings, the political living scenario, religious sentiments, the nocturnal social habitat,, along with you and me too is responsible for the crime.

Hence lets filter and participate in the inner sense of the religion in common and applying in our social systems and cleanse the society.

Mistakes due to social set-up of life styling and the social evil under any governance or any evil at a personnel place or abode or as situation raised at any instance regardless of the surrounding of personal condition may be main reason behind the victimization to sentence. Hence the society has direct or indirect responsibility to undergo the stress out of it or released by the stress to show empathy towards victims, It is advised to show mercy through extended sentencing or prolonged living time to repent and regain or repair the victim and access the feelings of the other peoples on the victim at a later stage.

So death is not the ultimate solution to any problems, even in the society. The society itself has to undergo a social surgery in its social set-up and regulations.

YOU ARE HUMAN BEING AFTER ONE THOUSAND LIFE CYCLES OF BIRTH & DEATH WE BELIEF SO....HENCE HUMANISM AT FIRST....

Its again time to make harsh rules and hanging as a prime punishment for the rapists of juveniles, well contained too. But is that the situation to be. Have you really ever studied the rules and ordinance to be announced. Should you have to appease the diseased and country men to show your mighty governance. The mightiest government t have already dried by doing so. The dirtiest tthallibaan had to laid down. The hangings in public/the slaughter in public/the stone pelting in public is pre-historic and its too is in union with the so-called terror outfit.

Can a intellectual, well educated, well qualified, elite, highly diplomatic society be so cruel to its own people on earth. Are there no other way to go, as the punishment is only death till now from pre-Jurassic era. Can we humans make a change intellectually. Even in this era of adulteration/livelihood adulterated and of moral instability. Even when we eat food we had great religious sentiments to gear us and guided us unquestioned. Its time that we rethink lest mankind be extinct. Humanism must be at forefront and not weapons or nuclear junks and armed arsenals.

India the moral society since long though history we know it. So religious, pious, *THE BEST MORAL* and social set-up, with the Vedic sutras OR SLOKAS chanting and dependent of spiritual life and the first to announce "Ahimsa Paramodharma" is stakeholder in this issue.

The diversified people of unity. Divine water logs flowing into the seas and oceans. Thus we are to start with the newest and neatest and clean weapon for punishment. No eye for an eye. No shoot-outs, no hangings by law or legal systems or governance or rebellious groups.

Hence to introduce a new method of punishment. We must get ready by heart and our mindset. We are to judge that the punishment must be a recoverable method to divert the culprit from his state of cruelty and crime to a state of honorable human being. He must be taught and self styled again to be away from crime. He must become a perfect human being and not just annihilating him from this earth.

Sending away or ejecting or squeezing a soul out of the body must be called a crime, say either suicide or killing by other means.

So we must find a new method or adopt new way or system that has to be called Funnishment and not punishment. Yet not a crime in disguise of law. It must make him feel guilty and repent to his wrong ways. It must be lesson to the other being, that never attempts to do so again. It must wipe off criminal thought out of the minds of all human being. It must eradicate the system and the criminal behavior of every individual.

What could you suggest: …????

……

To be edited by you readers

STILL CLINGING TO THE OLD PUNISHMENT OF:

1. Dungeon and demoralization

2. Prison and demoralization

3. Life term and liberalization

4. Hanging and hiding crimes

5. Crucified and crusaded

6. Stone pelting and own sin covered

7. Shooting and hanging in public and iseeesees

8. Slaughtering in public and slavery in public

9. An eye for eye and never you can buy one

10. Guillotine and Gala kaat de (cut throat!)

11. Water chocking dams and Sultans lucky chain.??

12. Waging wars and suppressing thoughts.

So We Change Now To Ammend???

Every mindset has to change to bring in the moral values that made our forefathers live.

You have to change your mindset to be more positive thinking to upgrade our secular beliefs. The nation cannot survive until and unless society changes. It is the Dharmikatha which held us together as Dharam was inculcated into our genes and blood by the Lord. Hence this unity in all of these diversities. Religion from outside has influenced not us, But we have accepted it, as it was the same moral values that came repacked in a neat fabric and our Gods were also living Gods.

QUEST FOR QUESTIONS AND CLAIMS

How come the religions or concepts or rules or wisdom or the constitutions never sees a life sense in human beings. How come cruelty itself is self contained in the context of controlling the society or governing a society to live on the earth with co –ordinance and co-operation.

How can a society as a whole with rule and policies to come or the judicial system to be justified on the barbaric nature of handling a situation and how can we hang a man for crime, when the whole social set-up and social effort of co-existence is indirectly or even directly responsible for it.

Well you said that there has judiciary to handle a social evil, trial and prosecution has lead to full death sentence. If death is only and the only one, the last judge able prosecution method to control a social systems forward march or continuation. And that too if a crime is judged at any other countries social set-up on and any other countries social system.

Then I would question you what does judiciary means. and I question myself of what has to be the judiciary. How to implement a law or how to study a law to be effective to control evil in the society.

Whether it has to be interlinked with religious sentiments or spiritual aggregates and thus we find solace in the judiciary system and there is a pinch from the so called religious law set-up too.

THE JUDICIARY AND THE GOVERNANCE

The Judiciary must be the first CARETAKER and overseer of the national governance of any country

- ➢ The judiciary has to be supervisor and the captain for steering the right path of the citizen to live amicably with other counter parts.

- ➢ The judiciary has to be very prompt and strong in the sense of actions taken to the law abiding through the enforcement of peaceful orders with clauses to which could not or would not harm the individual human rights.

- ➢ The Judiciary is the tool and tool maker to safeguard the fences under the boundaries of community which is governed by the judicial law without iron-hand in the application process.

- ➢ The judiciary is the right person to handle the broken fence, bars or links and the posts which has been rusted or termite ridden and replace the same with suitable new laws.

- ➢ The judiciary will see that the policies or amendments carried out by any formed government at the parliament with majority or minority voting be scrutinized or implemented without parity only and whence clear human rights non-violation is in the purview and promotion of the same be not left to the lonely decision of the Majority government.

- ➢ The judiciary and chief justice of the nation is the super head and watch guard of any government formed by democratic way of election through hardcore hardware's and ensure no software or embedded media and other virtual reality be used to seat a government body in the Parliament. As law is the supreme, the social enforcement in living and assurance in living is to be the supreme.

- ➢ Every laws and orders, rules and regulations is a fence and its not the crop.

- ➢ Every moment the poles of the fence or the wall aggregates fall off or ruin or rusts we have to change the same to replace to accommodate the safety of the crop. Sometimes a hard concrete fence would replace it.

- ➢ So in Judiciary the crop that's the civilians are more important to the nationhood.

EXECUTING THE RIGHT LIVING

HOW CAN A MAN THINK OR EXECUTE A MAN WHENCE HE HAS THE SAME LIKENESS IN EVERY SENSE. ARE WE STILL THE SAME OLD STONE AGE HUMAN SACRIFICED COMMUNITY ARROUND THE WORLD WITH MODERN TECHNOLOGY TO SACRIFICE HUMANS.

AND STILL WE BUILD A KNOWLEDGE CITY AND INFORMATION SUPER HIGHWAYS TO PARK OUR KNOWLEDGE. but where's

THE CHANGE IN INNER SELF???

Lets ward off all killings, hangings, shootings either political, governmental, military, monarchic or militant outfits.

As every one has the right to questioning any system, any dictation, any Government or monarchy, by verbal dialogues and they are answerable. Not under the law of the land but by humanitarian ground. No more suppression of questioning, speech or ideas though generated in the mind of common man too.

So change yourself by now to gain life to the ethical system of human civilized race which was defined by rulers, policy makers and by political process or monopolization of religious sentiments or all together.

Thus every killings must be counted and every Govt, is answerable also, even if punishable.

SO LETS CHANGE!?

LAW AND ORDER

Any killings by the Govt. or by law and order maintenance authorities are subject to be questioned and prosecuted by the peoples court. None has the right to shoot or smudge the peoples gathering for or against the Govt.. Instead the security and the safety shall be ensured by the Police and paramilitary or military to civilians. No surgical strike/sudden shoot out or death penalty can be implemented by the government on common people. Its the Governments duty to safeguard the interest and hear to their grievances on any protests against or questioning against any project and after effects or health hazards or community clashes and so on in due. As health and peoples wealth is most important in governance of an Nation. Life expectancy should be increased and Government has to do it with available resources and facilities available in the country. Human life is the most important in a collective peoples civilized land or empire. One individual can live in even in isolated land with no laws and selfless living styles in no mans land. All refugees can be in this separated land in a particular country and the individual can re-enter at certain periods back to old abode to live within the law of the land.

PEOPLES GATHERING

The peoples gathering shall be maintained by checking in through vio-cards given through the Government. agencies to the organizers and the team leaders for any protest or agitation or propagation or a promotion of an event at any instance or period of fasting or Dharna or struggle or Sathyagraha.

The no. of cards issued shall be equal to the gathering. Responsibility with all necessary security checks and returned in safe custody of the Government, agency after the events is vested in the organizers.

Any misrepresentations/any violence/any damage to public or private property or any government. or non-government property or shall be made accountable and responsibility shall be on the organizers; where in any indulgence can be taken proper action against the organization or party or person leading the event.

Adhar linked or embedded for specific period is to be done on vio-cards and deleted once the program ends.

RESOURCES AND SHARED LIVING

All resources shall be shared by all humans without borders and predetermined limitations. Everyone has the right to use resources on the earth with right proportion without harming the surroundings and harmony and nature of it.

No one person shall behold on to monopolize any resources of nature or intellect in character.

As intelligent was a net product of their effort of all humans race with due research or reform and intellects of centuries throughout, so no more intellectual property and stake holds.

Its a combined effort and energy flown through the windows of all human race. So not be boasting of your achievement as it is duty towards human and its not obligation and its not your service. A selfless effort put into work is seen in the wisdom quotient.

The self esteemed credibility is also seen in the cultured wisdom. Though there are differences in applicability. The inherent co-efficient of the effort all put together is called the knowledge or intellect. So be flexible in thoughts for the generation and the generation to come.

MORALITY AT DOMINANCE

Societies must be based on moral ability and moral stability of any country with dominance of moral value are to be considered. Hence the growth index has to change from per capita income to per morale outcome of the religious base, the spiritual tenders, and social pretenders are to be considered as a whole to generate growth index. The sanathana dharmik evolution is the social evidence through centuries passed on to this generation has to be considered.

But not on the grieve relevance of particular community based hindrances or particular religious sentimental preferences. it must entitle the gross liability to the society as a whole in building harmony or state of reliable in-built harmony among human.

So value based society that is provocative and promote human moral and harmony with individual and collective synthesized and synchronized social development must be called the growth index of potential morality.

It is not a rigid social binding but flexible rubber band of social kindness and compassionate background of the society.

SO LETS CHANGE!!!!

STOP MANUFACTURING OF WEAPONS

Only mutual talks and stakes must be at the first place to solve a situation so raised, whether its weapons of mass destruction or weapon of mass extinction.

The achievements in space and earth must be reflected through humanism. Each and every one has a stake hold in the achievements directly or indirectly even if its unclaimed. So every law and abiding it too has the stake hold to all humans, through humanism, though unclaimed. First change policies, change the rules, change the way to react and interact. Its counseling's that can change humans behaviors. Its the duty of the Government and not any other outfits and religion to take care. No more killings, no more hangings and no more shootings of any human by govt. or individual or animals too.. No more jails or dungeons or concentration camps or punishment chambers, Guillotine, no lock-ups for humans. All must change into counseling therapy centers and social behavioral correction centers, to change human beings from becoming animals.

Civil rehabilitations centers shall be established in every town.

So stop manufacturing weapons to be high and be the mighty powers. Even stop manufacturing pistols, riffles and guns for personnel use too. Its Government, duty to look into peoples safety. Whether individual or collective mass or community by means of day to day solutions to every one through countering the situations of any individual of community by officials at every village and community centers for counseling and calming the hearts through regular interaction as may situation a rise.

As you have no right to kill by law or through governance of personnel fist and fest.

SO LETS CHANGE!!!

Neither we have or any country has no right to question the existence of any individual in a country or any place surviving his natural adaptable conditions favoring his existence on this earth. But any one or any country can co-exist with the individuals only. Human individuality is not out of context & content. Its not exclusive product of the nativity. It is inclusively protected product of any place on the earth or universe. So no one has the right to bring inclusive and exclusive policy on any individual human or any race or sect or creed at any instance. So accommodating under inclusive nomenclature and natural habitat to be the prime motto of any society or civilized group of people whether monarchy or kingdom or parliamentarian rule established governance or democratic governance.

HENCE WE HAVE TO CHANGE!!!

ON THE LAST SENTENCE OF REPRENTATION

ALAS!! YOU TOO RUINED

No blasts can bring back any religious states neither your intentions of creating a unique religious state or any such nationalism is a fully illuminative vision of the crude thoughts of degenerative principles adopted from vein cultureless thoughts out of the context of a spiritual and religious being or self SINCE CENTURIES.

So once a collective degenerative thought arises that too organized crimes surface to annihilate the unwanted unsolicited ones to make way for the self esteemed group of intimidates.

And the very sense of insecurity in ones own solace is another thought of degeneration with backward march in civilized united living styles or establishments.

No thrash or lynching can accommodate a preventive method of holding stake in claims of beliefs that forsake humanism.

Every beliefs, faith and thoughts were raised by humans alone by intervention of the divine or once own innate or awakenings or wisdom.

Without humans alive no one can postulate his ideals or promote or propagate ones beliefs or faith.

Without the existing or coming or expected generations of human beings no ideology or spirituality or beliefs system can be implemented or enforced upon.

NO RELIGION OR A BELIEF SYSTEM OR THOUGHTS HAS GAINED INTO THE ROOT RATHER THROUGH HUMAN THAN ANY OTHER ANIMALS.

No spirituality was claimed by any source of outer conscious or inner subconscious senses to bring goodness and cheer in human hearts without humanism explained or exclaimed.

Hence lets be thorough and be thoughtful in energetic sense of human values, credentials and rights as a human.

Hence lets be clear through our hearts to impulse and judge the motivation of humanism into one another at every inch of life.

Hence lets be aware of the goodness of life that we are at stake and claim to live together amicably at any instance and place

Since generations have killed a lot and shed blood a lot, lets be the first human generation with technology and science, the elite and intellectual, enlightened beings of homo sapiens to stop all types of killings.

AHIMSA PARAMODHARMA!!!

NON –VIOLENCE IS THE ULTIMATE RELIGION!!!!

OHM SHANTHI! OHM SHANTHI!! OHM SHANTHIHEEE!!!

SATHYAMEVA JAYATHEY!!